Mitnick was known for his ability to manipulate people into giving him information.

HACKERS: BEHIND THE CODE

12 INCREDIBLE STORIES ABOUT FAMOUS HACKERS

Table of Contents

Kevin Mitnick Turned from *Bad to Good*

1

Many of us think we know about hackers. They use computers to steal information. Then they sell it on the black market. But many hackers don't fit this type. Kevin Mitnick is a great example. He's one of the most famous hackers. He was on the FBI's Most Wanted List in the 1980s. He broke into 40 companies just for fun. In some cases, he did it simply by calling up the companies. He tricked people into giving him usernames and passwords. This is called **social engineering**.

In 1995, Mitnick broke into one too many systems. He was caught and went to jail for five years. After his release, Mitnick changed his ways. He became a white hat hacker. That's someone who uses their hacking skills for good. They improve security so that bad hackers can't break in. Bad hackers are called black hat hackers.

Mitnick started his own cybersecurity company. He helped many companies. Microsoft was one. He even helped the FBI. He helped protect their information from hackers. Social engineering is still a problem. Mitnick helped train and educate companies around the world. Mitnick became a cyber celebrity. He was a bestselling author and speaker. He was often interviewed in the news. His story was featured in a movie called *Track Down*. Mitnick died of cancer in 2023. He left a lasting legacy. He showed people that black hat hackers can turn good.

CAT AND MOUSE Who finally caught Kevin Mitnick? Tsutomu Shimomura. He was an even better hacker. He is known as an **ethical** hacker. He helped the FBI find Mitnick, which led to his arrest. A book and movie were made about the takedown. The story inspires others to use their hacking skills responsibly.

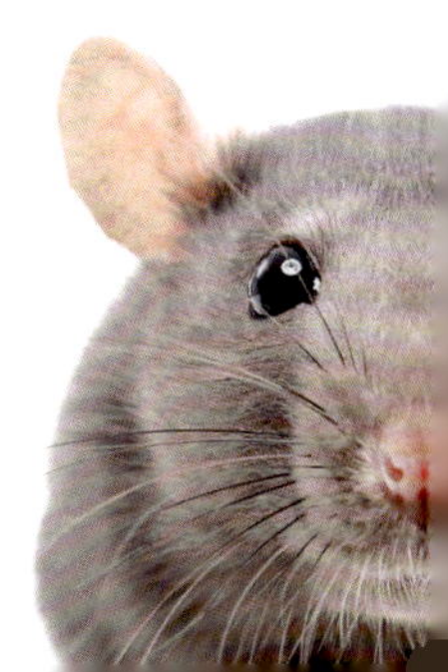

Jude Milhon Fought for *Equality*

2

Born in 1939, Jude Milhon was a hippie in the 1960s. She fought for civil rights and women's rights. She even went to jail in 1965 for organizing a march for voting rights for Black Americans.

Milhon taught herself to program in 1967. Soon she started working as a programmer in New York City before moving to California. In the 1970s, she was involved in the Community Memory Project. This was a way to post information on early computers. Frustrated by how few women there were in tech, she encouraged them to join the sector. Her motto was "Girls need **modems**!"

From the 1980s until her death in 2003, she turned to journalism. Under the name "St. Jude," she was the editor of a magazine called *Mondo 2000*. It featured articles about hacking, technology, and **cyberpunk**

17 Percent of tech firms with a female CEO.

About 27 percent of women worked in tech in 2025. • That's up from 9 percent in the early 2000s. • Men in STEM jobs earn at least $15,000 per year more than women.

A young women connects wires to a modem.

culture. She also spent time hacking in bulletin boards and personal computers.

In 1995, she co-authored a book called *The Cyberpunk Handbook*. She wrote about hacker culture. She included what to read and how to dress. Her goal was empowering women. She invented the term "Riot Grrl" for fierce girls who like tech. She helped found Cypherpunks. This group talks about ways to protect privacy online. Milhon always encouraged women to find their place in the tech world. She led by example. She showed both men and women what was possible.

Think About It Women have worked hard for equality in the workplace. Think of a woman you admire for breaking barriers.

Ying Cracker Teaches *Young Hackers*

3

Ying Cracker is a famous hacker in Singapore. She calls herself an ethical hacker. She's also a cybersecurity engineer. Others call her a professor hacker. All three are right! That's because Cracker teaches wannabe hackers. She teaches basics things, like changing an IP address. She also teaches complex things, like breaking into high-security systems.

"Cracker" is not her real last name. She hid that well online. Instead, she goes by Cracker. It refers to her skill. She "cracks" software protections. This unlocks special features without paying. She became popular in the mid-2000s. She was first noticed on message boards for her looks. She even modeled for a magazine in 2017.

Cracker is still in demand today. She draws in the new generation. These young hackers want to learn her skills and techniques. Cracker believes that anyone can learn to hack. She works with companies too. She teaches in-person and online courses. Some of them are free.

Cracker believes in female hackers. She wants to show that they can contribute to the field. Female hackers are breaking barriers. They are reshaping the male-dominated field.

TRAILBLAZERS

In 2000, Raven Adler made history. She was the first woman to ever present at DEF CON. This is a yearly hacker convention in Las Vegas. Now she's a security consultant, lecturer, and writer. Another trailblazer was Joanna Rutkowska. She's a Polish cybersecurity expert. She founded a security services start-up. She also develops software to protect against hackers. She was named one of the "Five Hackers Who Put a Mark on 2006" by *eWeek Magazine*.

25 Percent of cybersecurity experts who were women in 2023.

The number may increase to 35 percent by 2031. • More movies are showing women in hacking roles. • Female hackers can bring unique perspectives to cybersecurity.

DEF CON hosts speakers and cybersecurity challenges, known as wargames.

Steve Wozniak's Hacking *Launched Apple*

4

Have you ever used an iPhone or Mac computer? Do you wonder who started the company? It turns out, Apple's cofounders were hackers!

Steve Wozniak and Steve Jobs were in high school in 1971. Back then, long distance phone calls cost a lot. The two friends had an idea. They built a "little blue box." It tricked phone companies into letting them make long distance calls for free. This was illegal. But they never got in trouble for it. They took their box to the University of Berkley in California. There, they sold it to students. It sold like crazy.

Wozniak enjoyed many adventures in hacking. He played pranks on friends and family. He was even expelled from college for hacking. But the success of the blue box gave the two friends confidence. In 1976, they cofounded Apple. Jobs credits their first invention.

Blue box designed and built by Wozniak and sold by Jobs before they started Apple.

23 million Number of Mac computers sold in 2024.

Steve Wozniak designed the Apple II model computer in 1977. • Featuring one central processing unit, it revolutionized the computer industry. • Today, the company is worth $3.72 trillion. Wozniak sold his shares in 1985.

"If we wouldn't have made blue boxes, there would have been no Apple," he said. Jobs died in 2011.

Today, Wozniak is considered a founder of the personal computer. He designed Apple I. He helped bring computers into people's homes. Woz, as he is known, is worth about $140 million. He gives money to charity. He created Woz U. It helps high school students learn about software and technology.

Woz was added to the Inventors Hall of Fame in 2000. He follows a simple formula for his life. Happiness equals smiles minus frowns. He says it's the key to a meaningful life.

Think About It

Is it possible to do a bad thing for a good reason? Can you think of a superhero or character in a movie based on this idea?

Adrian Lamo Pressured Companies *into Fixing Holes*

5

In the early 2000s, Adrian Lamo was called the Homeless Hacker. He slept at friends' places most nights. He launched cyberattacks from different locations. He broke into the computer systems of major companies. Some of them included Microsoft and Yahoo. But he was doing them a favor. He wanted to show companies their weaknesses. He even offered to fix their issues for free. This would prevent a black hat attack.

Lamo wasn't a complete do-gooder. He was known as a **gray hat**. If the companies didn't listen, he went straight to the media. He told them who he hacked and how. Lamo wanted to pressure them to fix their holes. But he also liked the fame and attention.

His actions caught up to him. He was caught hacking *The New York Times'* server in 2002. In 2003, he was sentenced to six months of house arrest.

In 2010, Lamo became famous for a different reason. US soldier Chelsea Manning **leaked** sensitive government documents. They were posted on WikiLeaks. Lamo turned her in. Fellow hackers called Lamo a snitch. They said he betrayed their community. His actions still fuel debates on ethics in hacking.

750,000 Estimated number of documents leaked by Chelsea Manning.

WikiLeaks publishes leaked documents from **anonymous** sources. • After turning Manning in, Lamo's life went downhill. Hackers hated him. • Lamo died in 2018 at age 37.

During his hacking, Lamo found vulnerabilities in Microsoft's software.

Capital One lost the trust of many customers after Thompson's data hack.

Paige Thompson Stole Data *from Millions*

6

Paige Thompson was a software engineer. She worked for a **cloud** hosting company in Seattle. It was used to store sensitive information for big businesses, including Capital One. This is America's seventh largest bank.

Thompson knew about a weakness in Capital One's network. She used her hacking skills to **breach** their system in 2019. She stole information from 100 million customers. This information included credit scores and bank account records. She caused more than $250 million in damage. It was one of the biggest data breaches ever.

Thompson, then 33, couldn't wait to brag about it on online platforms. When Capital One realized what had happened, they contacted the FBI. In 2019, cyber investigators tracked down Thompson. They used the trail of information she'd left online. The FBI got a search warrant. They busted into her home and found the stolen information. Lawyers believed she was going to leak the data.

Thompson was charged with several crimes. She was found guilty in 2022. She served about 100 days in prison. Then she was given five years of **probation**. The case was a wake-up call for banks. They had to do a better job of securing their information.

A BIG IMPACT A lot changed after the Capital One breach. Capital One had to hire more tech people. They did a better job of safeguarding data. As of 2023, all public companies are required by law to have a plan to protect information. They share this each year with the Securities and Exchange Commission.

140,000 Number of social security numbers Paige Thompson stole.

She also stole 1 million Canadian Social Insurance numbers. • The US government fined Capital One $80 million for failing to protect data properly. • The victims sued Capital One for $190 million.

Jonathan James Was the First US *Teen Hacker Jailed*

7

Jonathan James was a computer genius from Florida. He taught himself computer programming and coding. At age 15, he decided to test out his skills. He did some "harmless exploration." He described himself as "curious." Some call him a gray hat hacker. Others say he is a black hat.

James gave himself the ultimate challenge. He wanted to hack into the US Department of Defense and NASA. He was successful. He found a back door and broke into their system. He tried telling the government how it. Nobody responded. But soon the FBI showed up at his door. They searched his home and took his computers.

James was charged with cybercrime. He was found guilty in 2000 at age 16. James became the first **juvenile** to be jailed for a US cybercrime.

James used the codename "c0mrade" when hacking high-profile systems.

$1.7 million Amount James cost NASA when he stole their source code.

This code let him attack their computers. • James was sentenced to six months in a juvenile detention center. • He was under probation until he was 21. • He also had to write apologies to NASA and the Department of Defense.

In 2008, James gained attention again. He was investigated for another cybercrime. The Secret Service raided his house. He was afraid he would end up in jail again. Sadly, he took his own life. His tragic ending shows the pressure of cybercrimes. But James is also known for his good deeds. He taught organizations to better protect their networks.

The Secret Service investigates financial crimes as well as protects important leaders.

Gary McKinnon Searched *for Aliens*

8

Gary McKinnon is a Scottish hacker. In 2001, he was in his London apartment. He hacked into the US Department of Defense and NASA. Using the name Solo, he searched around for months. He copied files and passwords. He messed up the network for days. What was he looking for? McKinnon wanted to find out about UFOs. He thought they had information. While searching, he left messages. "Your security system is crap."

McKinnon was arrested in London in 2002. He was age 36. He committed the biggest military computer hack of all time. The US government tried to bring him to the United States to stand trial. He could have gone to jail for 70 years. But after a 10-year legal battle, the United States lost its case. McKinnon had Asperger's syndrome. He was at risk of hurting

The House of Representatives oversees and funds the Department of Defense and NASA.

himself. The UK government thought sending him to America would go against his human rights. In the end, the UK government did not press charges against McKinnon. The case was dropped.

Today, McKinnon has a small business. He likes to write and record music. His story is being turned into a movie based on a book his mother wrote. The book is about their legal battle to keep him in the United Kingdom.

9 Gummo Got Rich Hacking *Smart Cards*

Gummo was born in Jacksonville, Florida. He says he grew up "dirt poor." He and his two older brothers were raised by a single mother. She dad died suddenly when Gummo was 12. Computers became his outlet.

Gummo taught himself how to code. He even set up a bulletin board at age 14. There he met other hackers. They taught him hacking tricks. He learned how to get free phone calls and other things. By 15, he was reprogramming credit cards. He used them in stores and at ATMs.

In 1989, Gummo lived in his car. He was 17. His girlfriend encouraged him to get a real job. She told him to leave his criminal work behind. But Gummo needed money to support his family. At a hacking conference in Germany, he discovered smart card systems. A smart card is a chip that can control access to phone lines and TVs. Gummo masterminded a scheme. He re-programmed DirectTV access cards. Then he and a partner sold the cards. Gummo earned $10 million before he was caught.

Gummo had the option to go to jail or work in cybersecurity. He chose security. He was thrilled to have a real job. Soon he protected companies from hackers like himself. Gummo ended up doing well for himself. He built four supercomputers to mine bitcoin. Using legal means, he mined 80,000 coins. Now he has about $7 billion.

2 Number of stock exchanges that Gummo helped protect.

Gummo first learned to code on a Tandy TRS-80 Model II computer. • The car Gummo lived in as a teenager was a 1982 Chevrolet Chevette. • In the 1990s and 2000s, the government often hired hackers like Gummo.

Credit cards are often targeted by hackers.

Albert Gonzalez Worked as a *Double Agent*

10 Albert Gonzalez pulled off the greatest credit card theft in US history. His rise to fame began in 2003. He got caught taking money at an ATM with stolen cards. To avoid charges, Gonzalez became an **informant**. He helped take down his old crew. While working for the Secret Service, he learned about cybersecurity. He learned its weaknesses. He saw a chance to commit his biggest crime yet.

It happened between 2003 and 2008. Gonzalez worked on an operation he called "Get Rich or Die Tryin'." While helping the government catch criminals, he also continued his own cybercrimes. He took banking information from big companies. These included OfficeMax, Target, and Barnes & Noble. Then he figured out how to resell more than 180 million credit card and ATM numbers. The Secret Service

$2.8 million
Amount Albert Gonzalez stashed away between 2003 and 2008.
He bought a condo in Miami, a car, several Rolex watches, and a Tiffany ring. • An additional $1 million in cash was found buried in his parents' backyard. • His crimes cost companies about $200 million.

learned of his double cross. They arrested him in 2008. His actions affected millions of people and businesses.

Gonzalez faced more than a dozen charges. These included computer fraud, conspiracy, and identity theft. He was sentenced to 20 years in prison. He was just 28 years old at the time. One government lawyer warned other criminals. "Today's sentence should serve as a warning," he said. Gonzalez was released in 2023.

Think About It

Has anyone ever stolen something from you? How did that make you feel? How does that make you want to treat others?

Robert Tappan Morris Creates *the Worm*

11

In 1988, Robert Tappan Morris was a 23-year-old graduate student. He studied at Cornell University. He was an expert in computer science. Morris developed a virus that could infect computers. It was called the Morris Worm. It multiplied itself across the internet. The internet was new at the time. This "worm" paralyzed computers.

When Morris released the virus, it spread to research labs. NASA was affected. So were universities like Harvard, Princeton, and Stanford. Within the first 24 hours, about 10 percent of computers were affected. That was 6,000 of the 60,000 computers. The disruptions cost up to $10 million.

A year later, Morris was charged for his crime. He was the first to be charged under the new Computer Fraud and Abuse Act. During his trial, he said that he wanted to show that current computer networks weren't safe. Morris was sentenced in 1990. His case made computer experts realize they had to take cybersecurity seriously.

Morris was released in 1995. He created a successful business. He sold his start-up company for $49 million. Then he went back to school. He got a PhD at Harvard. He now works at MIT in Boston. He teaches computer science and artificial intelligence.

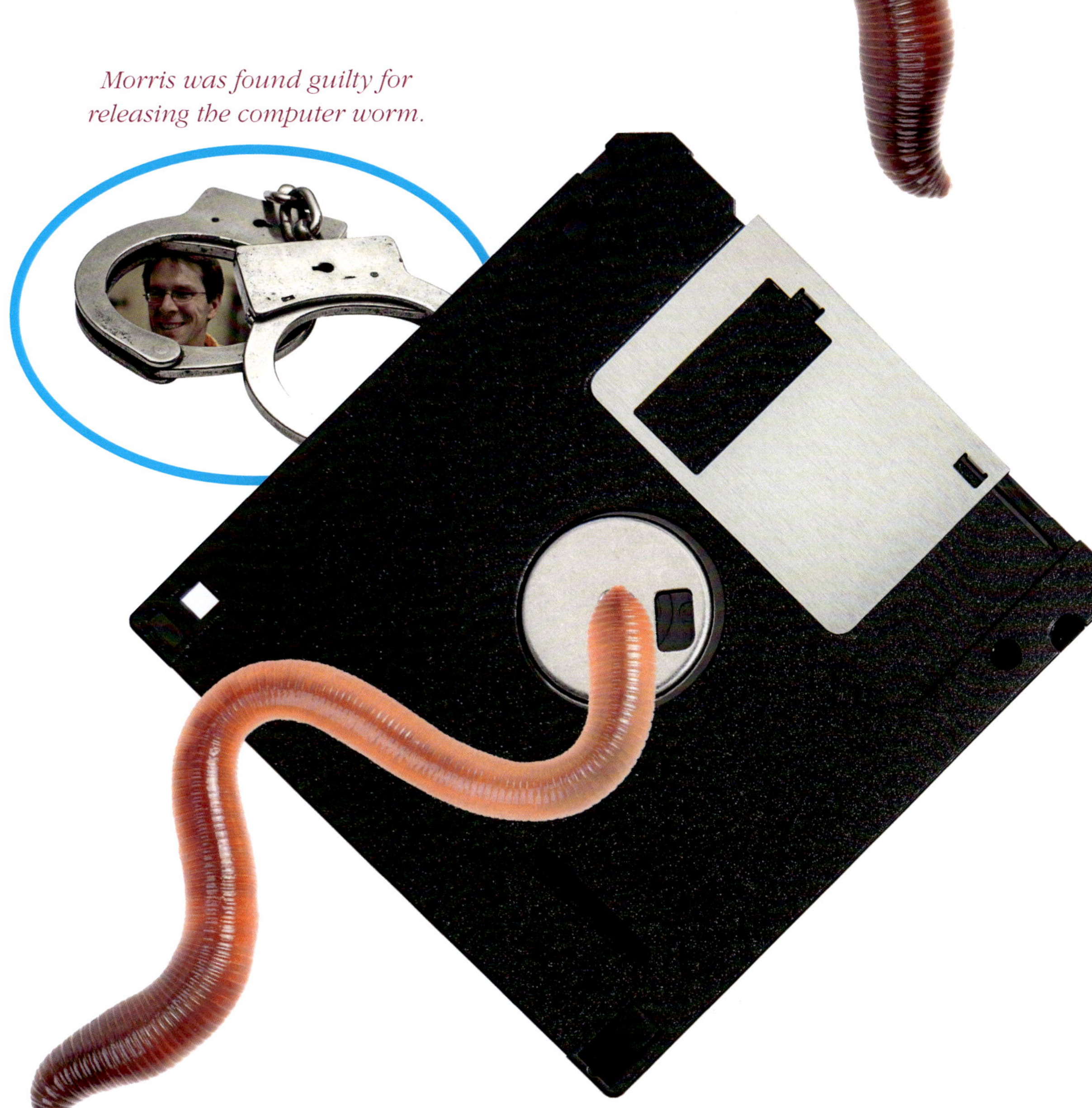

Morris was found guilty for releasing the computer worm.

GET TO KNOW GIGABYTE A female hacker was also known for her worms. Her real name is Kim Vanvaeck. She goes by Gigabyte. This Belgian hacker created havoc in the early 2000s. She launched high-end viruses. Infected computers had tell-tale signs of her work. They deleted files. A fireworks display might pop up. Or the screen would show messages with her views on hacking. Gigabyte was arrested in 2004.

Kevin Poulsen Turned from Hacker *to Journalist*

12

Kevin Poulsen was a teenage hacker. He was 17 when he was first caught. He had hacked into the Pentagon. He was warned not to do it again. But Poulsen didn't listen. He hacked into other government systems. He broke into phone networks. Poulsen was called a black hat hacker.

Poulsen hacked his way to winning a Porsche.

His most famous hack was in the early 1990s. He took over all the phone lines of a radio call-in contest. Poulsen won $20,000 and a Porsche car. But he didn't drive it for long. Soon, he was featured on NBC's *Unsolved Mysteries*. Poulsen went **underground** for 18 months. But it didn't help. He was caught in 1991.

Poulsen was convicted of computer fraud. He served about five years in jail. He was also banned from using a computer. He realized a life of cybercrime didn't pay. So he found a way to make it pay—legally. He became a respected reporter. He investigates cybersecurity and breaks major cases. He's worked for news organizations like *Wired* and the *Wall Street Journal*.

His investigative reporting made a big impact. For example, he used MySpace to find sex offenders in 2006. This led to arrests and policy changes at MySpace. It also led to new government legislation. In 2012, he released a book. It's called *Kingpin: How One Hacker Took Over the Billion-Dollar Cybercrime Underground*. Using his hacking knowledge, he helped create SecureDrop. This is a safe way for **whistleblowers** to get important information to journalists. Poulsen now lives in California with his family.

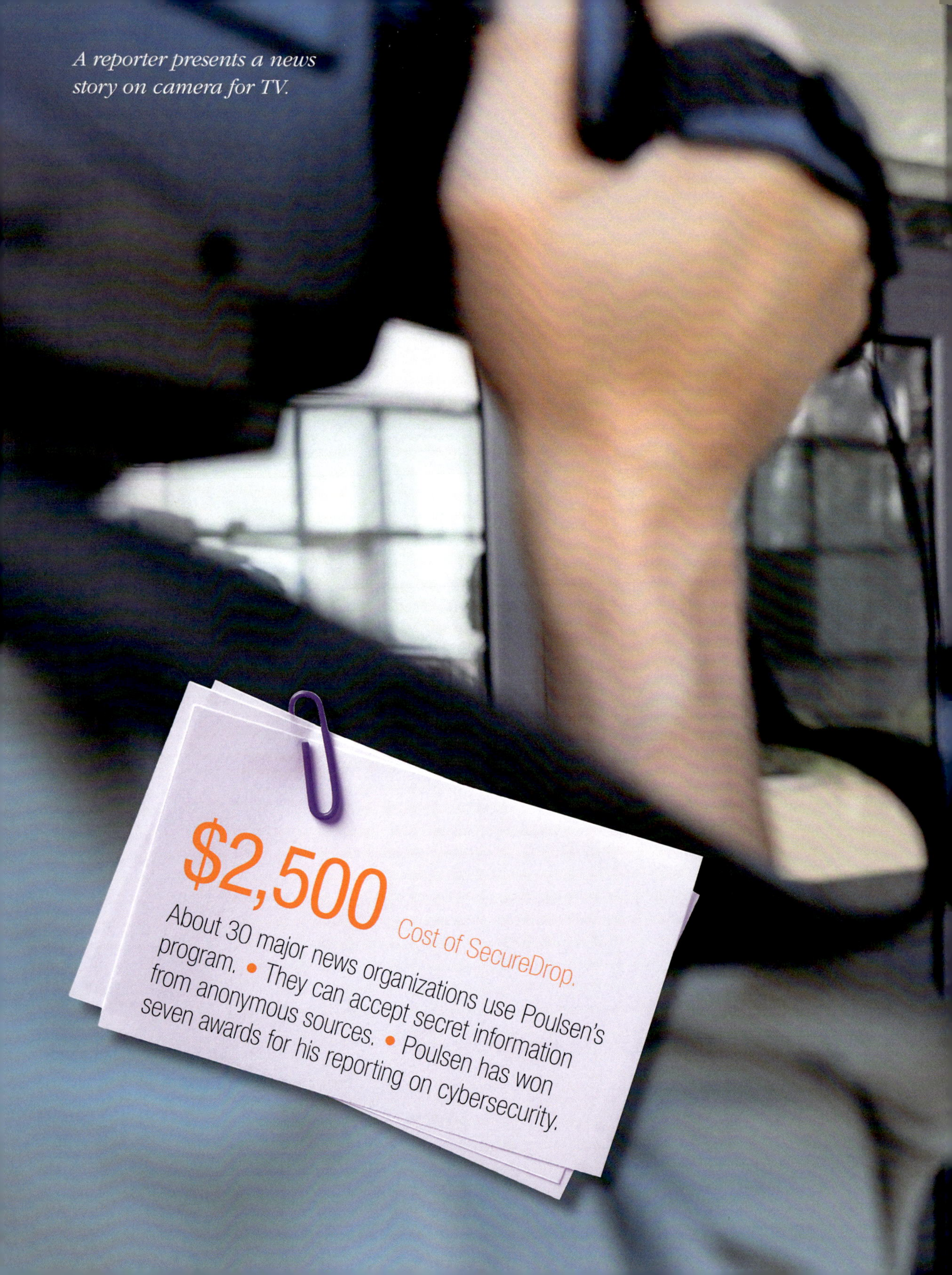

A reporter presents a news story on camera for TV.

REPORTING ON CYBERCRIME Are you interested in computers and journalism? You might want to be cybersecurity reporter. Investigating these criminals can be dangerous. But exposing threats and protecting information can also be exciting. Plus, it's rewarding. Start by getting a college degree. Study computer science, cybersecurity, criminal justice or journalism.

Fact

- One cyberattack occurs every 39 seconds. That's more than 6 billion attacks a year globally. In 2012, the United States had 447 data breaches. That number was 3,200 in 2023.

- Most successful cybercrimes are the result of weak passwords. Some are re-used or stolen passwords. Hackers tend to target people who work, learn, or play online.

- Hackers cost people a lot of money. The average cost of a cyberattack is $4.88 million. In the United States alone, cyberattacks cost $9.36 million each. Globally, cyberattacks were estimated to cost $10.5 trillion in 2025. This number may grow by 15 percent each year.

password:
123456
Don't forget to
change it!

Sheet

- About 95 percent of bad hackers are motivated by money. Most cyberattacks are organized by groups. They work together to plan and carry out big attacks. From 2021 to 2025, more than $1.75 trillion was spent on cybersecurity around the world.

- Female hackers are rare. And black hat female hackers are even more rare. It's impossible to estimate how many there are. That's because hackers tend to use code names.

- Susan Headley was one of the first female hackers. She was involved in a phone hacking scheme in 1977. She was 17 years old.

Glossary

anonymous
Not named or identified.

breach
A gap in a barrier or defense where someone can attack.

cloud
Large computers you can connect to on the internet and use for storing data.

cyberpunk
A resourceful computer hacker.

ethical
Following accepted rules of behavior.

gray hat
A hacker who may do unlawful or unethical hacking to achieve their purpose, sometimes for a good reason or personal gain.

informant
A person who gives information to the police about secret or criminal activities.

juvenile
A young person who is not old enough to be legally considered an adult.

leak
A situation in which people learn about information that is supposed to be a secret.

modem
A device that changes the form of electric signals so that information can be sent to computers through telephone lines.

probation
A period when a criminal is allowed to stay out of prison if they behave well.

social engineering
The use of lies and psychological influence to get someone to sharing secret or private information that may be used for unlawful purposes.

underground
In a place that is hidden or secret.

whistleblower
A person who tells police or reporters about something that has been kept secret.

For More Information

Books

Eason, Sarah. *Hunting a Hacker: Using Science to Crack Cybercrime.* Shropshire, UK: Cheriton Children's Books, 2023.

Hudak, Heather C. *Cybercrime.* Minneapolis: Abdo Publishing, 2020.

Payne, Bryson. *Go H*ck Yourself: A Hands-On Introduction to Hacking.* San Francisco: No Starch Press, Inc., 2023.

Miller, Michael. *Cyberspies: Inside the World of Hacking, Online Privacy, and Cyberterrorism.* Minneapolis: Twenty-First Century Books, 2021.

Websites

The Infamous Masterminds: A Look into the World of the Top 20 Famous Hackers
bluegoatcyber.com/blog/the-infamous-masterminds-a-look-into-the-world-of-the-top-20-famous-hackers/

Kevin Mitnick: The World's Most Famous Hacker
www.mitnicksecurity.com/about-kevin-mitnick-mitnick-security

The Secret Lives of Hackers
tpt.pbslearningmedia.org/resource/nvcy-sci-slhackers/the-secret-lives-of-hackers/

About the Author

Erin Silver is an award winning children's author and freelance writer based in Toronto, Canada. She loves learning about new technology and the power of AI. Visit her at ErinSilver.ca.

Index

TOP RANK is published by Black Rabbit Books, P.O. Box 227, Mankato, MN, 56002. • Designed by Danny Nanos • Photographs © Associated Press/Eric Risberg, 2, 16; Dreamstime/Oleg Palium, 41, Stangot, 45; Getty Images/imaginima, cover, 1, Kimberly White, 2–3, Mel Melcon, 4, Westend61, 9; Shutterstock/artstore, 44, Ascannio, 22, Belinda Pretorius, 48, Bing Wen, 12–13, Chirawan Thaiprasansap, 39, DenisNata, 45, divdevelopment, 20, Elnur, 24, FotoDax, 21, Georgy Timoshin, 44, Hans-Joachim Roy, 11, happiness time, 39, HJBC, 18–19, hsagencia, 37, 38, 39, Ivan Cholakov, 40, Jolygon, 46–47, Kuttelvaserova Stuchelova, 7, lev radin, 27, LightField Studios, 42–43, mikeledray, 26, MVelishchuk, 36, Nithid Memanee, 30, Phonlamai Photo, 23, PrinceOfLove, 28, Przemek Klos, 29, Radu Bercan, 40, RODWORKS, 34–35, Roman Samborskyi, 10, Runrun2, 2, 16, Sanit Fuangnakhon, cover, 1, Shuttertum, 31, Sonsedska Yuliia, 6–7, Stas Malyarevsky, 8, Valeri Luzina, 32–33; Wikimedia Commons/Federal Bureau of Investigation, 5, Juanglassford, 25, Maksym Kozlenko, 15, Trevor Blackwell, 39, U.S. Probation Dept./public domain, 17 • Printed in the United States of America.
Library of Congress Cataloging-in-Publication Data: Names: Silver, Erin, 1980- author | Title: 12 incredible stories about famous hackers / by Erin Silver. | Description: Mankato, MN: Top Rank, [2026] | Series: Hackers: behind the code | Includes bibliographical references and index. | Audience: Ages 9–13 | Audience: Grades 4–6 | Identifiers: LCCN 2025021474 (print) | LCCN 2025021475 (ebook) | ISBN 9781645825258 library binding | ISBN 9781645825432 paperback | ISBN 9781645825616 ebook | Subjects: LCSH: Hackers—Juvenile literature | Computer crimes—Juvenile literature | LCGFT: Literature | Classification: LCC HV6773 .S55 2026 (print) | LCC HV6773 (ebook) | DDC 364.16/8—dc23/eng/20250709